Hey Fam! Success is Here

Written by Tiffany Dean

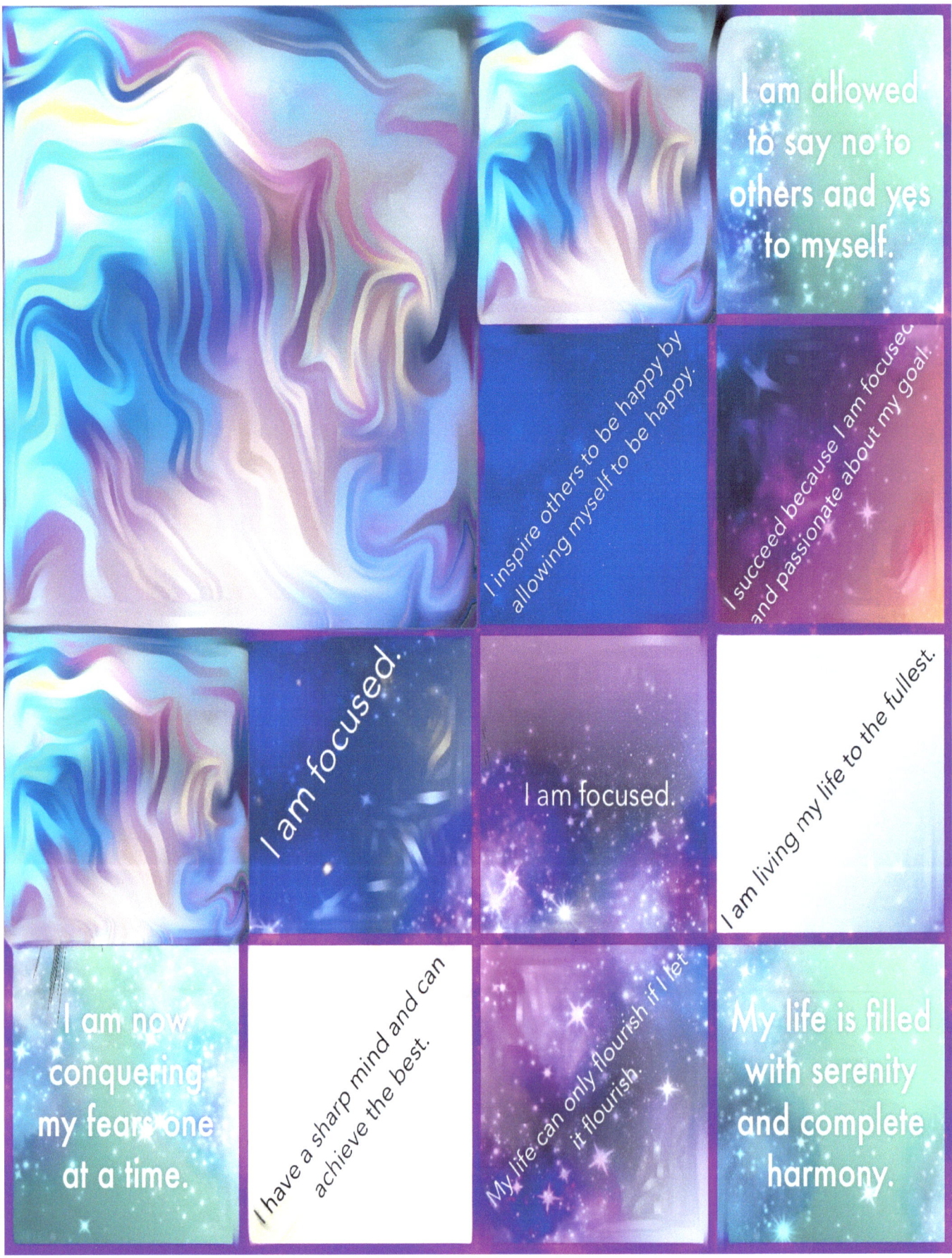

Dedication

This book is dedicated to all of the children in the world. It's dedicated to everyone who needs hope and encouragement. This book is dedicated to my Daybreak kids and to my #1 son. This book is dedicated to Love.

Connection

When my pen hits the paper,

My soul starts to speak,

My mind starts to wonder,

Then my pen starts to leak.

The words from my heart,

Are written on these lines.

Words I can not speak out loud,

Just flowing thru my mind.

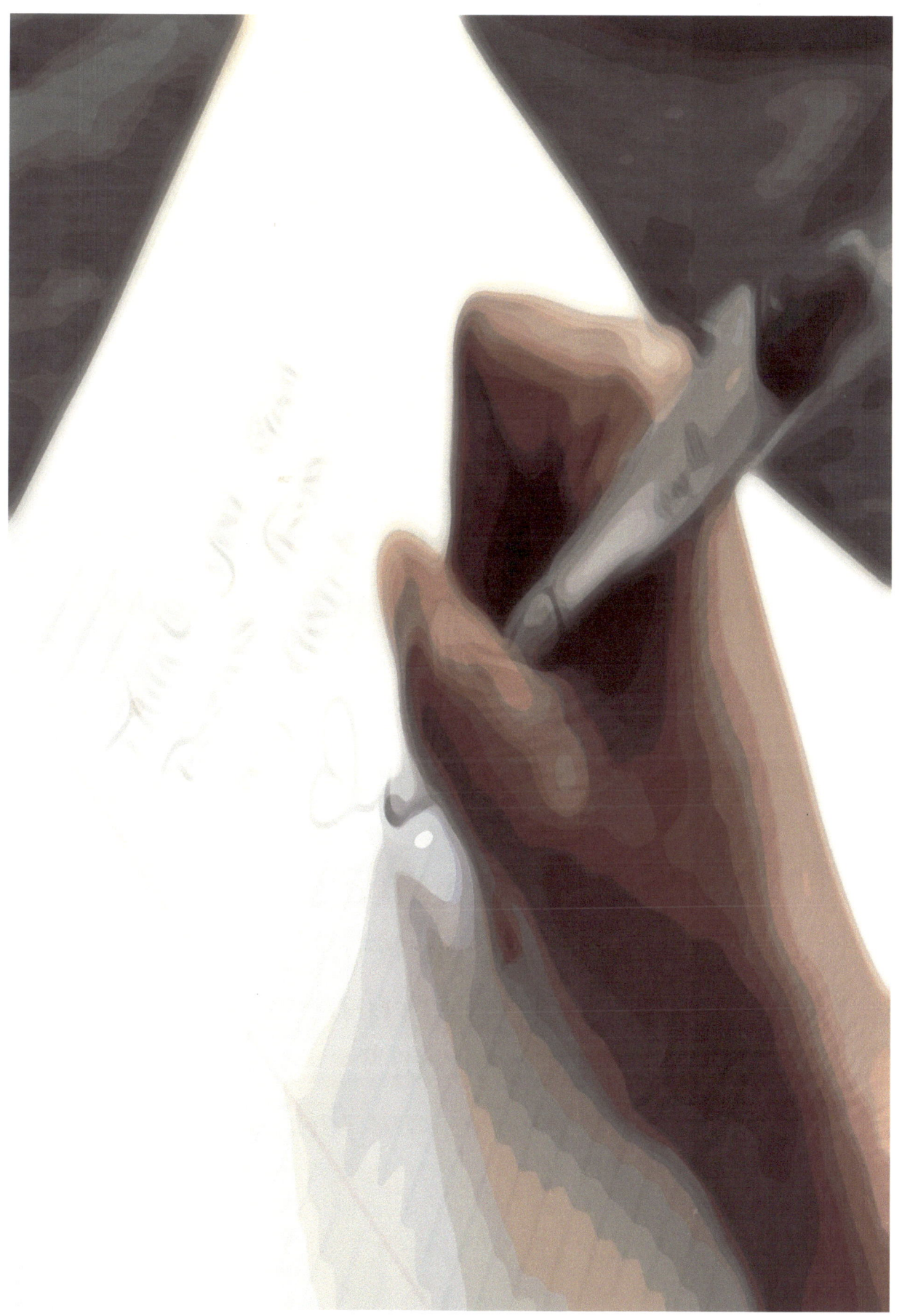

LIKE A STORY

Life is like a story being told.
When you wake up a new chapter will unfold.
There are challenges you take,
To find out what will be your fate,
But only time will tell you how the story goes.
To strive and achieve are My goals.
Strive for my life.
Achieve my dreams
And
Heal my soul.
Sometimes I feel like giving up,
I feel as if I have no luck.
Then God says, "Everything is under my control"
And that makes me feel whole.

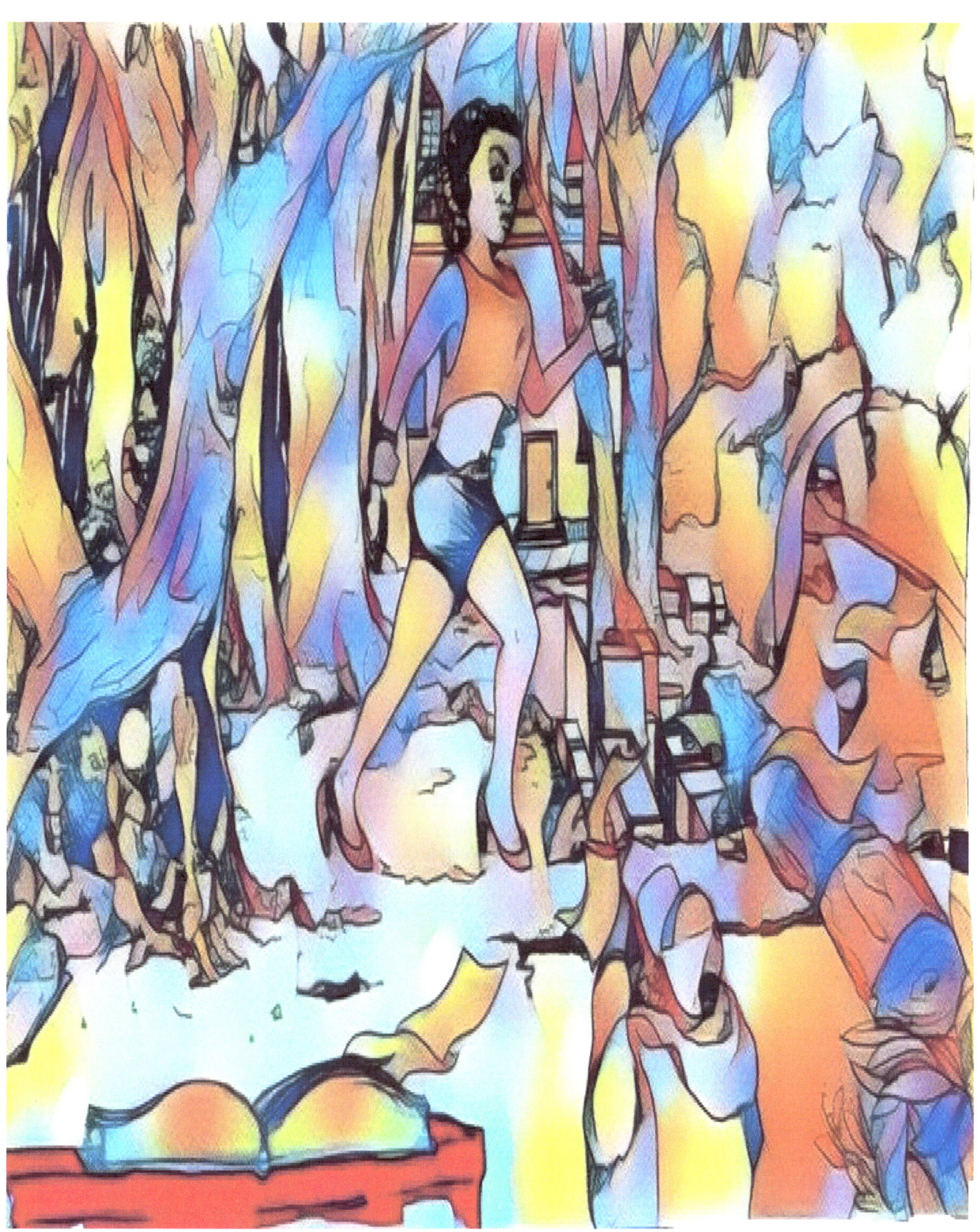

Love Yourself

First you gotta love yourself
Then love God and know your wealth
Love your kids and protect them
Love life like it's a precious gem
No one can make you happy but you
And no one can do things quite like you do
So focus on your goals and never look back
Focus on God and you'll stay on track
Don't worry about a man or a woman
Cuz they can't get you into heaven

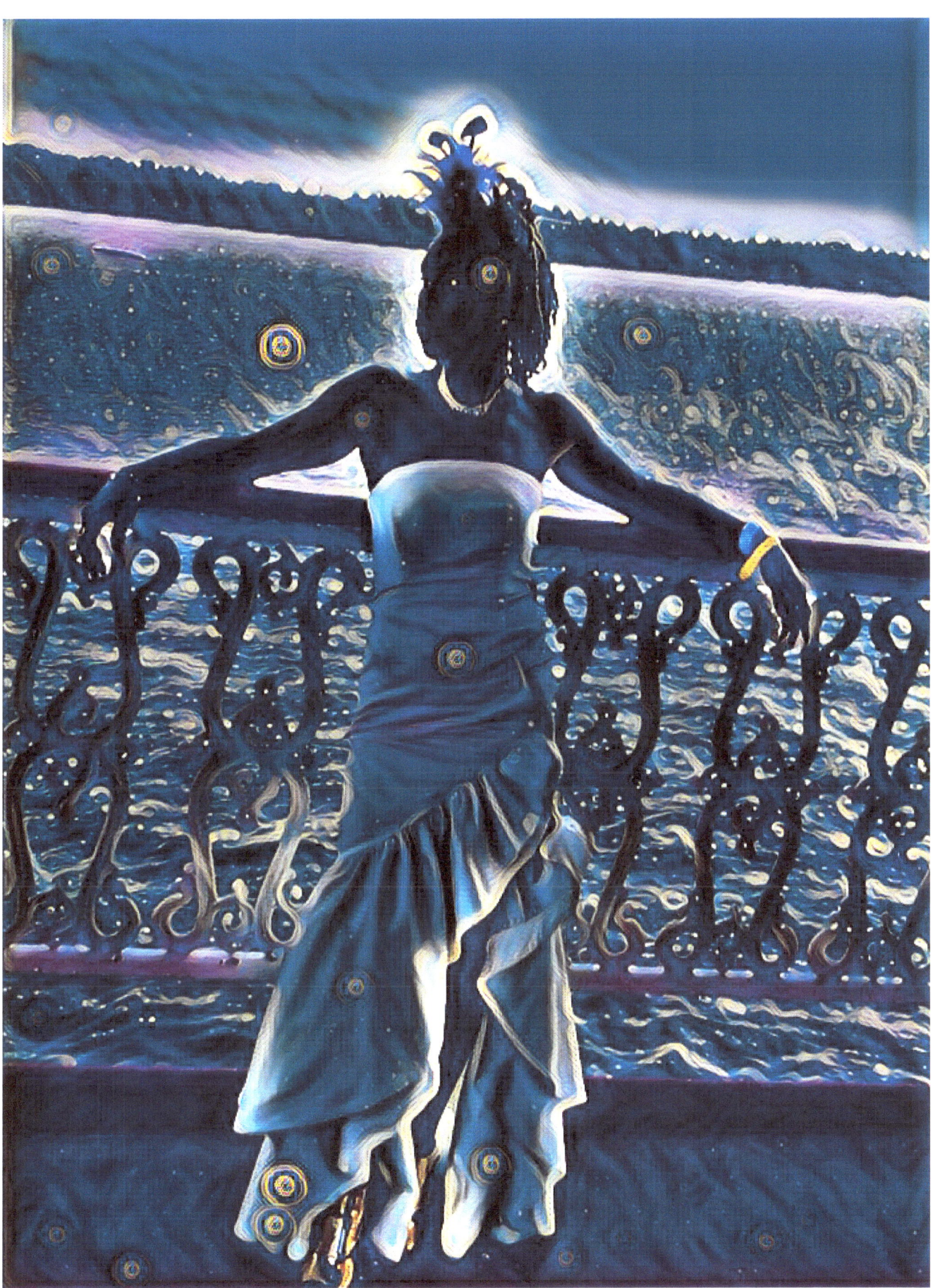

I WILL

I will Accomplish my goal with every strength in my Soul

I will Live up to my dreams for my heart knows what it Means

I will Always be okay because the Lord will make a way

I will Be just fine because there's always still time

To make it right, and to win the **fight**

To make things **better** even in the stormy weather

I will Succeed

I know *I will* Succeed

I will, I will, I will, I will, **I can Succeed**

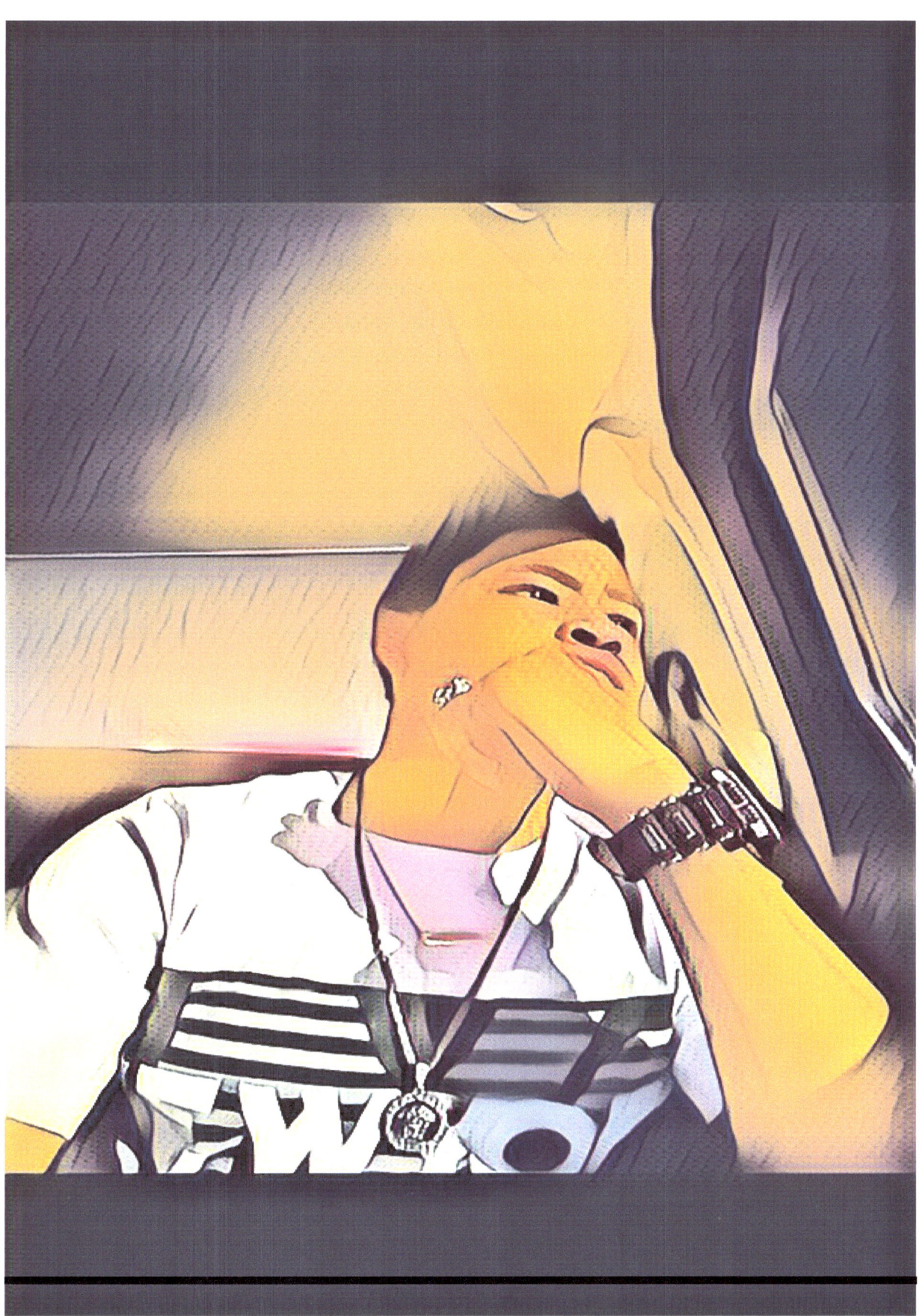

LEARN

Everything happens for a reason

Somethings are just for a season

Learn from every situation

And eliminate any complication

Trust in God and you will see

Just how simple life can be

So live and learn, and Don't give up

You must believe He'll fill your cup.

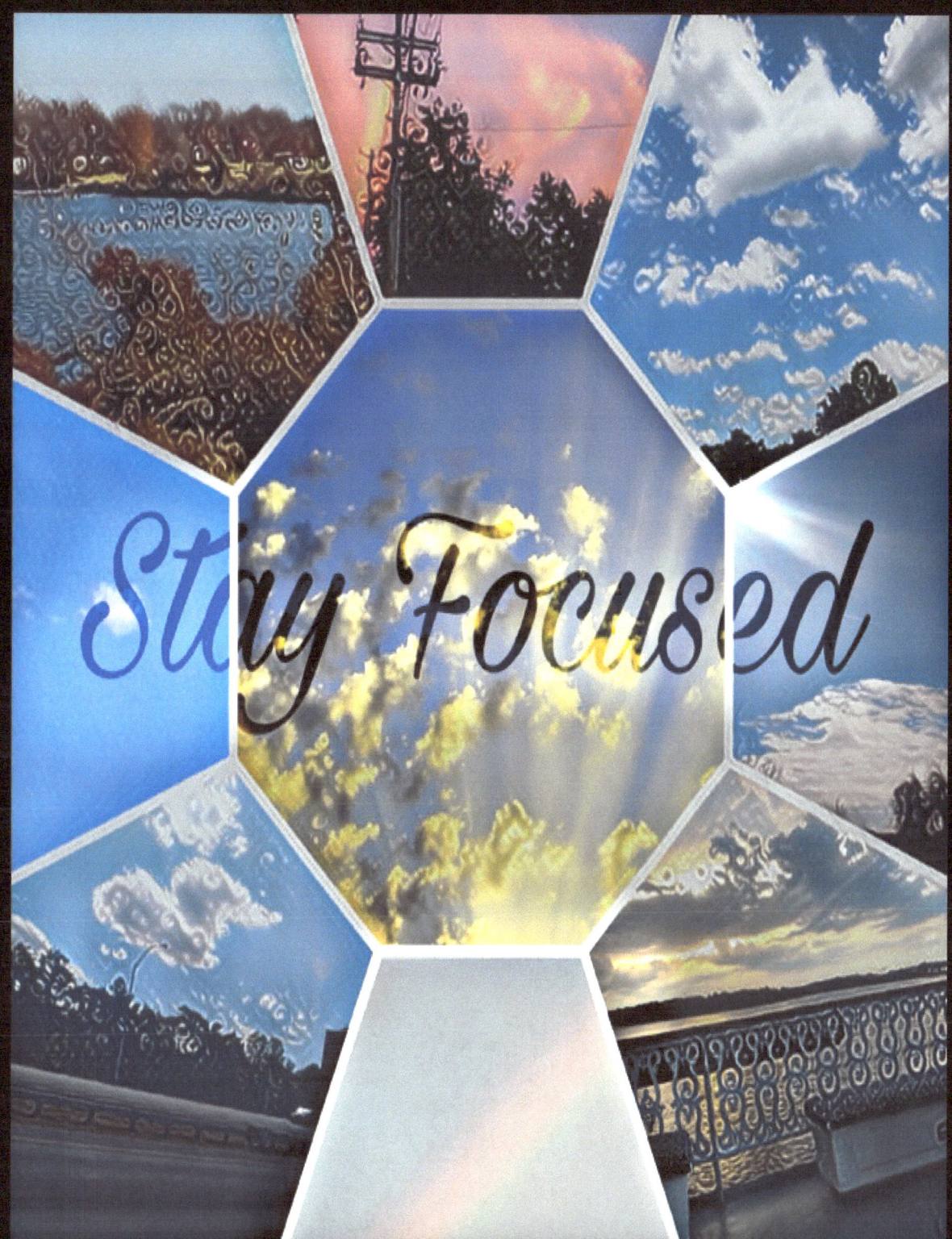

Who I am

Who am I?   *I am Intelligence*

Fierce and Strong, with passion and song.

My mind grows with knowledge,

I wonder and long

For peace

Who am I?   *I am Queen*

Respectfully created by the creator Himself

My flaws and curves makes me top shelf

Love, loyalty, and life live inside of me

Respecting the Crown that was given to me

Who am I?   I am Success

Hard work and determination are some traits

Accomplished dreams and goals are my fait

Unlimited opportunities fill my mind

Endless possibilities will come on time.

Who am I?   **I am that I am**

Imperfect, not perfect, but perfect for me

To love myself first, unconditionally.

To know who I am and who I'm meant to be

God makes no mistakes, So I'm here

And I'm ME

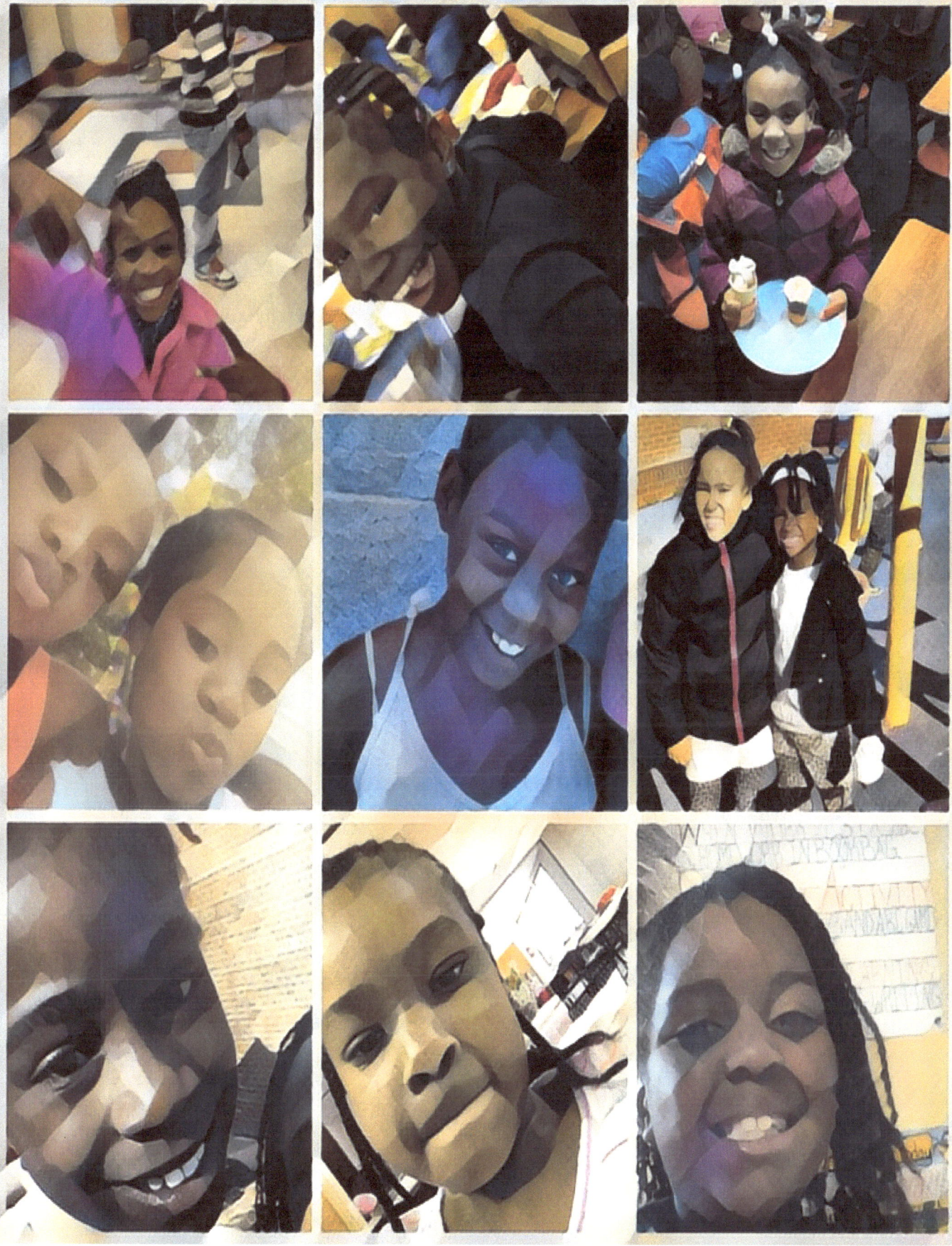

Who Will I Be

I will be a strong black man
A good man, A gentleman
I will be smart and intellectual
A God fearing man
I will walk God's walk and talk God's talk
I will change the world, and leave my mark
Whether I'm a doctor, lawyer, or a fireman
I will be the best man
I will be an honest man
Trying my best to follow God's plan
With family by my side, I know I will be okay
God watches over all of us every single day
I will help people, both old and young
If it is God's will, it will be done
I am the future and I want my future right
I'll do what I have to do to make my life bright

I Will be the best ME.

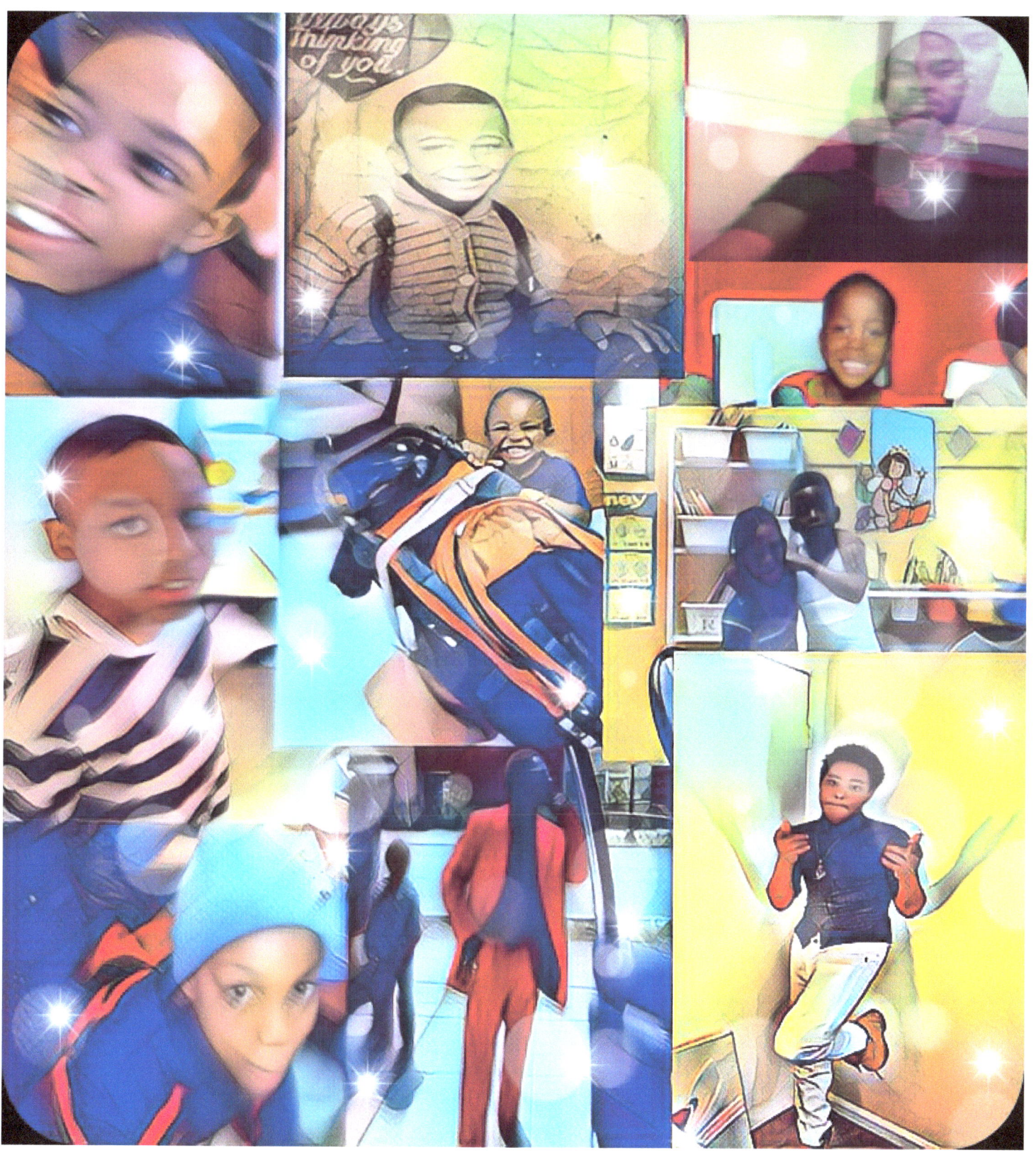

Who am I?

I am strong
I am confident
I am talented
I am ME
I am special
I am unique
I am crazy
I am ME
People don't understand me
People tend to hurt me
People come in and break my heart
But people have made me ME
God created me
God, He blesses me

God has put me thru some tests
To prove my loyalty
To prove that I can be
The best Me above the rest
To prove to God that   _(Say your name)_
Is ready to be free
I am protected
I am loved
By the Lord and family
I am ready to be Free
I am ready to be ME

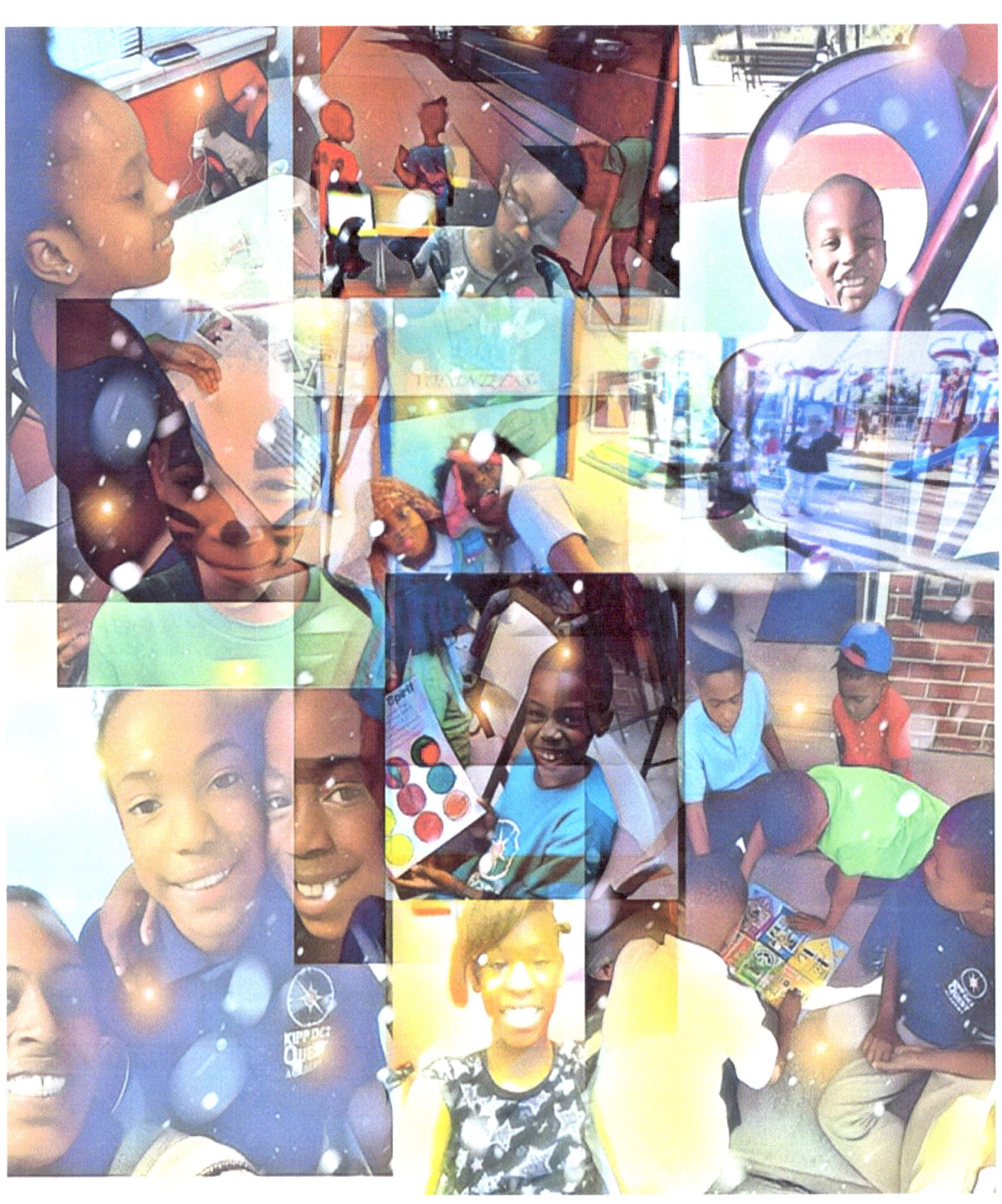

My God

I felt Him flowing through my soul
The words, He spoke them
They made me whole
He spoke my language
Yet I understood
That He was God
He is the mighty of Lord
I love Him dearly
He guides me through everyday
He gives me signs
To push the devil away
God tells me things
That no one else can hear
He guides me the right way
And helps me have no more fear

My God

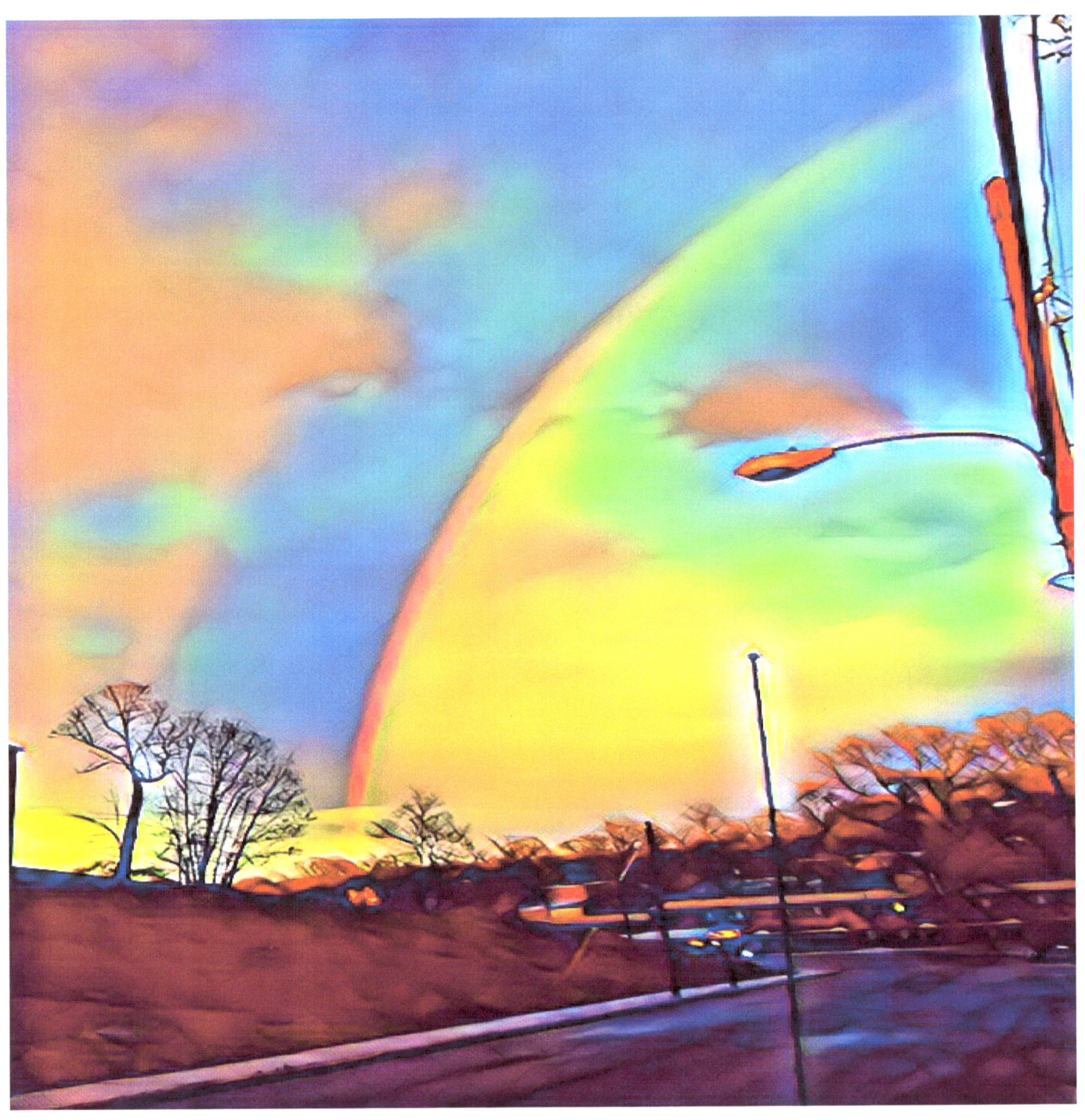

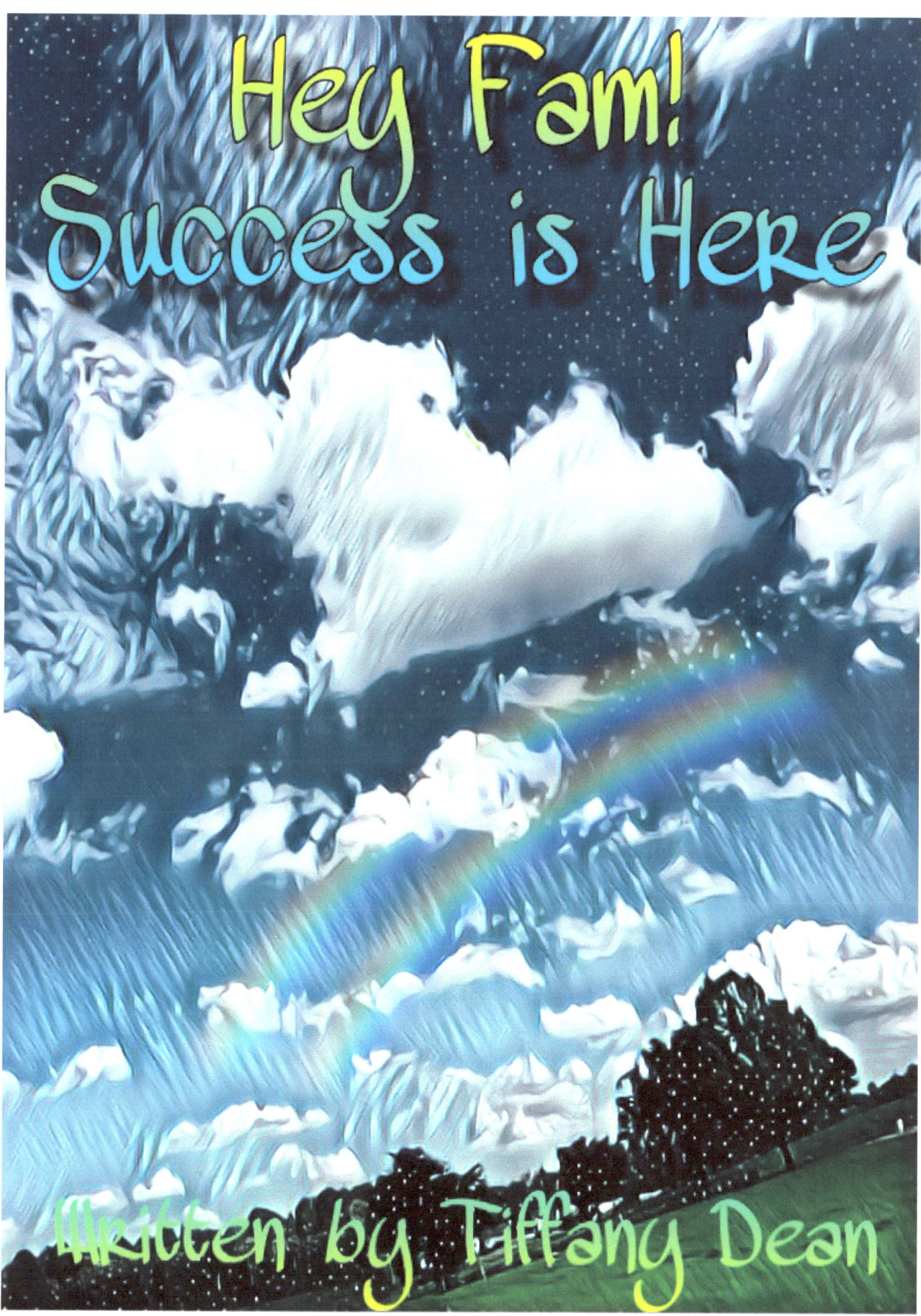

www.ingramcontent.com/pod-product-compliance
Lightning Source LLC
Chambersburg PA
CBHW051837210526
45473CB00005B/1916